cookies
biscuits
& biscotti

cookies
biscuits
& biscotti

LINDA COLLISTER

photography by

PATRICE DE VILLIERS

RYLAND
PETERS
& SMALL

LONDON NEW YORK

Art Director **Jacqui Small**

Art Editor **Penny Stock**

Editor **Elsa Petersen-Schepelern**

Photography **Patrice de Villiers**

Food Stylist **Linda Collister**

Stylist **Penny Markham**

Production **Kate Mackillop**

To Daniel

Notes: Ovens should be preheated to the specified
temperatures – if using a fan-assisted oven, adjust time and
temperature according to the manufacturer's instructions.

First Published in Great Britain in 1997
by Ryland Peters & Small
Kirkman House, 12–14 Whitfield Street, London W1T 2RP
www.rylandpeters.com

This paperback edition first published in 2003

10 9 8 7 6 5 4 3 2 1

ISBN 1 84172 533 1

A CIP record for this book is available from the British Library.

Printed and bound in China.

homemade biscuits **6**

traditional biscuits **10**

shortbread **20**

chocolate and nuts **26**

around the world **42**

fingers and bars **54**

index **64**

CONTENTS

homemade
biscuits

A homemade biscuit is a small luxury. It turns a coffee-break or a midnight snack into a moment of sheer pleasure – a little self-indulgence to warm your own day, or hospitality to brighten someone else's. Making biscuits is easy enough, but a few pointers may be helpful. Most importantly, you need good ingredients for good results. I always use unrefined, **pure cane sugars** (except refined icing sugar for decoration), because they have a slightly deeper flavour. Shown left, from top are demerara sugar, golden caster sugar, dark and light muscovado sugar, icing sugar and golden granulated sugar. I prefer **unsalted butter:** the taste is better and the cook, rather than the manufacturer, controls how much salt goes in the recipe. I also prefer medium or large **free-range eggs** and always use them at room temperature. They taste better and produce better results than battery eggs. **Organic and stoneground flours** are sold in most supermarkets – I use them because they are healthier and have better flavour. **Nuts** should be as fresh as possible: the oils they contain quickly turn rancid when exposed to air, so always store open packets in the freezer.

Use plain **chocolate** with at least 70 per cent cocoa solids: supermarket own-labels are usually of very good quality and value. Some of the recipes in this book use white chocolate – use best-quality, and not children's white bars. When using **lemon or orange zest**, use unwaxed fruit and wash the fruit well before removing the zest.

Best-quality **real vanilla essence** (the finest is from Mexico or Madagascar) should always be used. Because vanilla is expensive, some of the essence available is either low-grade or fake and chemical, and so smells and tastes very harsh.

It is worth investing in good tools – they make baking easier and more successful. **Accurate** scales and measuring spoons are essential. A teaspoon is 5 ml, a tablespoon 15 ml: all should be measured level unless the recipe calls for a rounded or heaped spoonful. **Electric food mixers** and processors don't just save time, they also make complicated recipes easier, less messy and less exhausting.

Biscuits scorch easily, so thin, cheap **baking sheets** can ruin the best recipe and the most careful preparation. Heavy, professional-quality sheets or those specially made for biscuits are wise investments and last a lifetime.

Airtight containers are vital for **storage** – biscuits quickly lose their crispness, and often their shape, in humid conditions.

An **oven thermometer** is also very useful (many thermostats are unreliable). Each oven is an individual – most are temperamental. Learn how yours behaves, how quickly it warms up, how well it retains heat and where the hot spots are. Baking times in these recipes cannot be more than guidelines, so know your oven, and watch your biscuits carefully. Check the manufacturer's handbook if you are using a fan oven, or for guidance on shelf positions.

TRADITIONAL **BISCUITS**

Two versions of a classic *biscuit.*
wheaten biscuits

170 g stoneground
wholemeal flour

a good pinch of salt

1 teaspoon baking powder

50 g porridge oats

40 g golden granulated sugar

100 g butter, chilled and diced

one 7.5 cm round biscuit
or scone cutter

several baking sheets, greased

Makes about 16

Put all the ingredients in a food processor and whizz until the dough comes together. (In very cold weather, you may have to work the lumps of dough together with your hands.)

Turn out the dough on to a lightly floured work surface, and roll out to about 5 mm thick. Using a 7.5 cm biscuit or scone cutter, cut the dough into rounds. Knead the trimmings together, re-roll, then cut out more rounds.

Arrange the biscuits on the prepared sheets and prick them well with a fork. Bake in a preheated oven at 190°C (375°F) Gas 5 for about 12–15 minutes until they turn colour slightly at the edges.

Remove from the oven and let cool on the baking sheets for 3–4 minutes until firm enough to transfer to a wire rack. Let cool completely, then store in an airtight container. Best eaten within 1 week, or freeze for up to 1 month.

Variation:
Savoury Wheaten Biscuits
Make the dough as in the main recipe, reducing the quantity of flour and adding the spices. Proceed as in the main recipe, and serve with cheese.

Reduce the granulated sugar in
the main recipe to 20 g

Add ¼ teaspoon curry powder or
garam masala, or 1 teaspoon of
ground cinnamon or ginger

Makes about 16

oat and raisin biscuits

Mix the flour with the salt, baking powder and oats.
Using a wooden spoon or electric mixer, cream the butter, sugar and vanilla until fluffy.
Using your hands or a wooden spoon, gradually work in the flour mixture and dried fruit, then knead the mixture until it comes together. Roll it into balls about 3 cm across.
Place the balls well apart on the baking sheets, then flatten them slightly with your fingers.
Cook in a preheated oven at 180°C (350°F) Gas 4 for about 10–12 minutes or until golden.
Cool on the baking sheet for a couple of minutes until firm enough to transfer to a wire rack.
Let cool completely, then store in an airtight container and eat within 1 week, or freeze for up to 1 month.

250 g self-raising flour

a pinch of salt

1 teaspoon baking powder

175 g porridge oats

250 g unsalted butter, at room temperature

200 g golden caster sugar

½ teaspoon real vanilla essence

50 g raisins, dried sour cherries or dried cranberries

several baking sheets, greased

Makes about 32

Make these biscuits with **dried sour cherries** *or* **dried cranberries** *instead of raisins – for an unusual and flavourful alternative.*

13

old-fashioned gingernuts

350 g self-raising flour

a pinch of salt

200 g golden caster sugar

1 tablespoon ground ginger

1 teaspoon bicarbonate of soda

115 g unsalted butter

85 g golden syrup

1 large egg, beaten

several baking sheets, greased

Makes 30

Sift the flour into a mixing bowl with the salt, sugar, ginger and bicarbonate of soda. Heat the butter and syrup very gently in a small pan, mixing occasionally, until the butter melts. Let cool until just warm, then pour on to the dry ingredients. Add the egg and mix thoroughly.

Using your hands, roll the dough into 30 walnut-sized balls. Place the balls well apart on the prepared sheets, then flatten slightly with your fingers.

Cook in a preheated oven at 170°C (325°F) Gas 3 for about 15–20 minutes or until golden brown. Remove from the oven and leave on the sheets for a minute to firm up, then transfer to a wire rack to cool completely.

Store in an airtight container and eat within 1 week, or freeze for up to 1 month.

*If you like gingernuts **chewy**, cook them for about 15 minutes until just firm – or if you prefer them **crunchy**, cook just a few minutes longer.*

A *traditional* biscuit from the *West Country.*

cornish fairings

100 g plain flour

a pinch of salt

1 teaspoon baking powder

½ teaspoon bicarbonate of soda

1 teaspoon ground ginger

½ teaspoon ground mixed spice

40 g golden caster sugar

50 g unsalted butter, chilled and diced

1 tablespoon mixed peel, very finely chopped

3 tablespoons golden syrup

several baking sheets, greased

Makes about 20

Sift the flour into a mixing bowl with the salt, baking powder, bicarbonate of soda, ginger and mixed spice. (The combination of the two raising agents is what makes these biscuits crack.)

Stir in the sugar. Add the cold chunks of butter and rub the mixture together with your fingertips until it resembles fine crumbs. Stir in the mixed peel, then the syrup, to make a firm dough. (In cold weather, warm the syrup after measuring, but before adding it to the mixture.)

Using your hands, roll the dough into about 20 marble-sized balls. Space them well apart on the prepared baking sheets.

Bake in a preheated oven at 200°C (400°F) Gas 6 for about 7 minutes or until golden.

Remove from the oven and let cool on the sheets for a couple of minutes. Transfer to a wire rack to cool completely.

Store in an airtight container and eat within 1 week, or freeze for up to 1 month.

Crisp, *light biscuits – great on their own, or a perfect complement to ice creams or fruit salad.*

lemon poppy seed
biscuits

200 g plain flour

a pinch of salt

50 g icing sugar

50 g golden caster sugar

the grated rind of 1 lemon

2 teaspoons poppy seeds

120 g unsalted butter, chilled and diced

1 medium egg, beaten

several baking sheets, lightly greased

Makes about 26

Put the flour, salt, sugars, grated lemon rind and poppy seeds into a food processor and combine thoroughly. Add the cold chunks of butter and process until the mixture resembles fine crumbs. Add the egg and process again until the dough clumps together.

Shape the dough into a log about 7 cm in diameter and wrap it in foil. Chill until hard – at least 2 hours, or up to 1 week. The mixture can be sliced and baked when needed.

When you are ready to cook the biscuits, slice the logs into rounds about 5 mm thick, and place them slightly apart on the prepared baking sheets.

Bake in a preheated oven at 180°C (350°F) Gas 4 until the edges are just beginning to turn golden brown – about 10–12 minutes. Transfer to a wire rack, and let cool.

Store in an airtight container and eat within 5 days, or freeze for up to 1 month.

grasmere
ginger shortbread

200 g plain flour

50 g fine oatmeal

1 teaspoon ground ginger

½ teaspoon bicarbonate of soda

125 g light brown
muscovado sugar

1 piece of stem ginger in syrup,
drained and roughly chopped

125 g unsalted butter,
chilled and diced

one 20 cm square tin,
well greased

Makes 9 squares

Mix all the ingredients except the butter in a food processor until they form the texture of coarse sand. Add the cold chunks of butter, then process until you have fine crumbs. Do not overwork the mixture – it should not form a dough.

Set aside 4 tablespoons of the crumbs. Tip the rest into the prepared tin and press them into an even layer with the back of a spoon. Sprinkle the reserved crumbs on top.

Using a round-bladed knife, score the shortbread into 9 squares. Bake in a preheated oven at 180°C (350°F) Gas 4 for about 25 minutes or until they are just beginning to turn golden. Remove from the oven.

Cut along the scored lines, but leave the shortbread to cool in the tin before turning out.

Store in an airtight container and eat within 1 week, or freeze for up to 1 month.

*A favourite shortbread recipe from the Lake District, with a strong **ginger** flavour and a **crumbly** topping, another with green unsalted pistachios and a third with **sugary** speckles.*

demerara shortbread

Using a wooden spoon or electric mixer, beat the butter until creamy, then beat in the caster sugar and vanilla essence, if using. Continue beating until the mixture is light and fluffy. Sieve the flour with the rice flour and salt, then add to the mixing bowl. Work the dough with your hands until it comes together, then knead gently for a few seconds.
Form the dough into a log shape 16 x 7.5 cm. Roll in the demerara sugar until evenly coated. Wrap in foil or greaseproof paper and chill until firm – about 20 minutes. Unwrap the log and slice into 1 cm rounds. Arrange slightly apart on the prepared baking sheets, prick with a fork, then chill for about 15 minutes until firm.
Bake in a preheated oven at 180°C (350°F) Gas 4 for about 15 minutes until firm but not coloured.
Cool for a couple of minutes, then transfer to a wire rack to cool completely. Store in an airtight container and eat within 1 week, or freeze for up to 1 month.

200 g unsalted butter, at room temperature

100 g golden caster sugar

2–3 drops real vanilla essence (optional)

260 g plain flour

40 g rice flour, ground rice or cornflour

a pinch of salt

3–4 tablespoons unrefined demerara sugar

one 7.5 cm round plain cutter
several baking sheets, greased

Makes about 16

Variation:

Pistachio Shortbread

Make the dough as in the main recipe, adding the pistachios but omitting the vanilla. Turn out on to a lightly floured surface, then roll out to 1 cm thick. Cut into rounds with the cutter, knead the trimmings together, re-roll and cut more rounds. Omit the demerara sugar. Arrange the rounds slightly apart on the prepared baking sheets, then chill for about 15 minutes until firm. Bake as in the main recipe.

Omit the vanilla and demerara sugar from the above ingredients, and add 50 g shelled pistachio nuts, blanched, dried and roughly chopped

Makes about 14

This rich, grainy shortbread is ***perfect*** *with vanilla ice cream.*
chocolate shortbread

Using a wooden spoon or electric mixer, beat the butter until creamy and light. Add the sugar and beat again until fluffy. Sift the flour with the cocoa and salt. Using a wooden spoon or your hands, work them into the mixture until it comes together. Knead gently for couple of seconds, then press the dough into the tin to make an even layer.

Cover and chill for 15 minutes. Prick the dough well and score into 12 sections with a round-bladed knife.

Bake the shortbread in a preheated oven at 180°C (350°F) Gas 4 for about 15–20 minutes – do not allow it to brown or it will taste bitter.

Remove from the oven, sprinkle with caster sugar, or icing sugar and cocoa, then cut into sections along the marked lines. Let cool before removing from the tin.

Store in an airtight container and eat within 1 week, or freeze for up to 1 month.

200 g unsalted butter, at room temperature

100 g golden caster sugar

260 g plain flour

40 g cocoa powder

a good pinch of salt

extra caster sugar or icing sugar, for sprinkling

one 23 cm round cake tin, greased

Makes 12 triangles

Only the **finest** *dark chocolate is*
suitable for this recipe.

bitter chocolate
butter biscuits

70 g plain chocolate,
roughly chopped (preferably with
at least 70 per cent cocoa solids
and very little sugar)

35 g golden caster sugar

220 g unsalted butter,
chilled and diced

140 g light brown
muscovado sugar

250 g plain flour

½ teaspoon real vanilla essence

50 g white or plain chocolate,
melted, to decorate

several baking sheets,
well greased

Makes 30

Blend the chopped chocolate and caster sugar in a food processor until they form the texture of sand. Add the diced butter, muscovado sugar, flour and vanilla, then process again until the dough just comes together.

Using your hands, form the dough into about 30 walnut-sized balls. Space well apart on the baking sheets.

Bake the biscuits in a preheated oven at 180°C (350°F) Gas 4 for 10–15 minutes or until they are just firm to the touch and beginning to colour around the edges.

Remove from the oven. They are very fragile at this stage, so leave them on the sheets for 5 minutes before transferring to a wire rack to cool.

When completely cold, decorate by drizzling with the melted chocolate using either a fork or a greaseproof paper icing bag. Leave until firm, then store in an airtight container and eat within 4 days.

Undecorated biscuits can be frozen for up to 1 month, but you may have to crisp them in a warm oven before decorating.

lace biscuits

Very gently melt the butter in a small pan, then let it cool while you prepare the other ingredients.

Blend the nuts, sugar and flour in a food processor until the nuts are finely ground. With the machine still running, pour in the cream and butter through the food tube. Process until you have a soft dough.

Space heaped spoonfuls of the mixture well apart on the baking sheets. Flatten them with a fork, then bake in a preheated oven at 180°C (350°F) Gas 4 for 7–9 minutes or until they turn golden brown with slightly darker edges.

Let cool on the baking sheets, then store in an airtight container and eat within 4 days. They do not freeze well.

These *delicate* elegant biscuits are perfect to serve with sorbet or little cups of strong, black, after-dinner coffee.

50 g unsalted butter

100 g chopped pecan nuts or walnut pieces

100 g golden caster sugar

3 tablespoons plain flour

2 tablespoons double cream

several baking sheets lined with non-stick baking parchment

Makes about 24

For **crunchy** *texture and intense almond taste, use freshly ground and whole nuts – toasted first – and real almond essence.*

almond crescents

120 g unsalted butter,
at room temperature

2–3 drops real almond essence
(not almond flavouring)

60 g icing sugar, sieved

a pinch of salt

90 g plain flour, sieved

120 g ground almonds

30 g whole almonds,
lightly toasted then chopped

extra icing sugar, for dredging

several baking sheets, greased

Makes about 22

Beat the butter and almond essence until light and creamy, Add the sieved sugar and, using a wooden spoon or electric mixer, mix slowly, then beat well until fluffy. Add the salt, flour and ground almonds, then mix thoroughly with a wooden spoon. Mix in the chopped toasted almonds and, if necessary, knead the dough gently, just enough to bring it together.

Do not overwork the dough – it should be quite firm. In warm weather, you may need to wrap it and chill for 15–20 minutes to harden the dough to the proper consistency.

Using your hands, roll heaped teaspoonfuls of the dough into sausages about 7 cm long, curving each into a crescent. Space well apart on the prepared baking sheets, then cook in a preheated oven at 170°C (325°F) Gas 3 for 15–18 minutes or until firm. They should still be pale, with only the tops slightly browned.

Let cool on the sheets for 2 minutes, then dredge with icing sugar. Transfer to a wire rack to cool completely.

Store in an airtight container and eat within 1 week. This recipe does not freeze successfully.

For the best flavour, make the **strongest** *possible espresso coffee, then let it cool before using.*

espresso
walnut squares

140 g plain flour

a pinch of salt

140 g light brown
muscovado sugar

90 g unsalted butter,
chilled and diced

1 teaspoon baking powder

1 medium egg, beaten

3 tablespoons very strong
espresso coffee, cold

1 tablespoon milk

60 g walnut pieces

one 20 cm square cake tin,
greased and base-lined

Makes 16 squares

Sift the flour, salt and sugar into a mixing bowl. Add the cold chunks of butter and rub with your fingertips until the mixture resembles coarse crumbs. Set aside 4 tablespoons of the mixture. Add the baking powder to the rest and mix well.

Combine the egg, coffee and milk, then stir into the mixing bowl. When thoroughly combined, add 45 g of the nuts. Spoon the mixture into the tin and level it.

Mix the remaining nuts with the reserved crumbs and scatter over the top.

Bake in a preheated oven at 180°C (350°F) Gas 4 for about 20–25 minutes until golden brown and firm to the touch.

Let cool for about 1–2 minutes, then run a palette knife around the edges of the tin to loosen it and carefully turn on to a wire rack.

Leave until completely cold before cutting into 16 squares. Store in an airtight container and eat within 4 days, or freeze for up to 1 month.

Always use **fresh** *nuts, good chocolate and* **strong** *coffee.*
mocha macaroons

Gently melt the chopped chocolate in a heatproof bowl set over a pan of barely simmering water. Remove from the heat and stir until smooth.

With a hand whisk or electric mixer, whisk the egg whites until they form stiff peaks. Gradually whisk in the sugar, then fold in the almonds, coffee and chocolate.

When well mixed, put heaped teaspoonfuls, spaced well apart, on the prepared baking sheets. Spread into circles about 6 cm across and decorate with the almonds.

Bake in a preheated oven at 150°C (300°F) Gas 2 for about 25 minutes or until firm.

Let cool, then peel off the parchment or remove them from the greased sheet. Transfer to a wire rack, and leave until completely cold.

Store in an airtight container and eat within 1 week. The macaroons do not freeze well.

75 g plain chocolate, chopped

2 medium egg whites

200 g golden caster sugar

125 g ground almonds

1 tablespoon strong espresso coffee

sliced, split or slivered almonds, to decorate

several baking sheets, well greased or lined with non-stick baking parchment

Makes 18

35

*Use **sugar-free** peanut butter in this recipe, or the biscuits will be much too sweet.*

peanut butter and jelly
biscuit sandwiches

275 g crunchy peanut butter

150 g golden caster sugar

2–3 drops real vanilla essence

1 large egg, beaten

about 4 tablespoons raspberry jam or red currant jelly, for the filling

several baking sheets, well greased

Makes about 12 sandwiches

In a mixing bowl, beat the peanut butter and sugar together, then beat in the vanilla essence and the beaten egg. The dough should be very stiff.

Divide the dough into 24 pieces and roll them into balls with your hands. Space the pieces well apart on the baking sheets, then flatten with a fork.

Bake in a preheated oven at 180°C (350°F) Gas 4 for about 12–15 minutes or until golden brown. Leave them on the sheets for a few minutes to firm up, then transfer to a wire rack until completely cold.

Sandwich pairs of biscuits together with a little jam or jelly. Store in an airtight container and eat within 1 week.

The biscuits can be frozen for up to 1 month, but they must be frozen without the jam or jelly filling.

Note: *this recipe is suitable for people on gluten-free diets, and for serving during Passover.*

*An **elegant** combination of white nuts, white chocolate and a white biscuit mixture.*

white chocolate
macadamia nut crumbles

200 g plain flour

a pinch of salt

½ teaspoon baking powder

175 g unsalted butter,
at room temperature

100 g golden caster sugar

1 medium egg, lightly beaten

½ teaspoon real vanilla essence

150 g good quality white
chocolate, coarsely chopped

75 g unsalted macadamia nuts,
coarsely chopped

several baking sheets,
lightly greased

Makes about 24

Sieve the flour, salt and baking powder into a bowl.

In another bowl, cream the butter and sugar until fluffy using a wooden spoon or electric mixer.

Beat in the egg and, when thoroughly mixed, stir in the flour mixture with a large metal spoon. When no streaks are visible, stir in the vanilla, chocolate and nuts.

Put tablespoons of the mixture, spaced well apart, on the prepared baking sheets. Bake in a preheated oven at 180°C (350°F) Gas 4 for 10–12 minutes until firm but not coloured.

Leave the biscuits to cool on the sheets for a minute, then transfer to a wire rack to cool completely.

Store in an airtight container and eat within 5 days. These biscuits do not freeze well.

Walnuts make wonderful biscuits, but **pecans** *or* **hazelnuts** *will also work well in this recipe.*

walnut biscuits

70 g walnut pieces, chopped

90 g unsalted butter, at room temperature

80 g golden caster sugar

80 g unrefined demerara sugar

1 large egg, beaten

½ teaspoon real vanilla essence

250 g self-raising flour

several baking sheets, greased

Makes 24

Walnuts can sometimes be very bitter, and can also turn rancid very quickly when exposed to air, so taste one first before using them in this recipe.

Using a wooden spoon or electric mixer, beat the butter until soft and creamy. Gradually beat in the sugars and continue beating for another 2 minutes.

Beat in the egg a little at a time, then stir in the vanilla, flour and chopped nuts. Work the mixture with your hands until it comes together into a firm dough. Again using your hands, roll the dough into 24 walnut-sized balls.

Space them well apart on the baking sheets, then flatten with a fork. Bake in a preheated oven at 180°C (350°F) Gas 4 for about 10 minutes or until golden and firm.

Leave on the sheets for a couple of minutes to firm up, then transfer to a wire rack to cool completely.

Store in an airtight container and eat within 1 week, or freeze for up to 1 month.

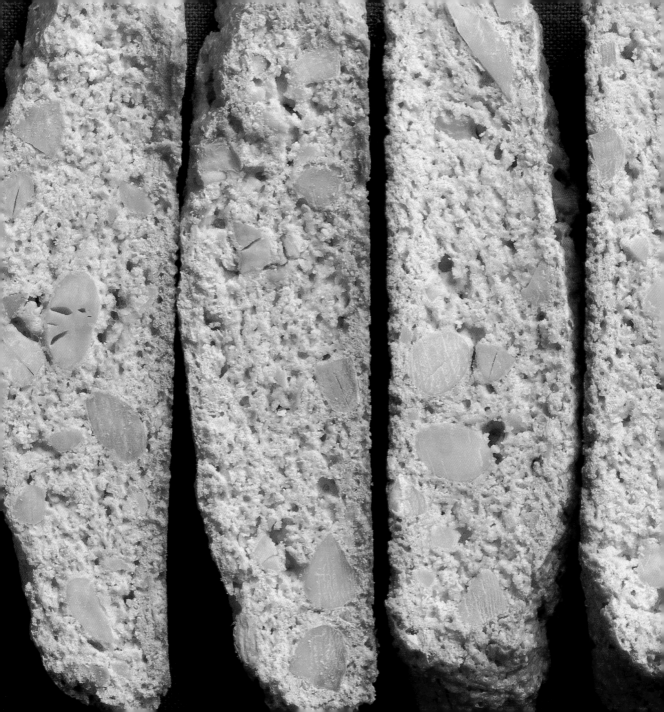

almond biscotti

130 g blanched almonds

250 g plain flour

125 g vanilla caster sugar, if available, or caster sugar

¾ teaspoon baking powder

2 large eggs, plus 1 yolk

½ teaspoon real almond essence or vanilla essence

a baking sheet, greased

Makes about 20

These twice-baked biscotti from Tuscany are served after dinner with fresh fruit and a glass of sweet **Vin Santo** *wine for dipping and sipping.*

Toast the almonds on a heatproof dish in a preheated oven at 180°C (350°F) Gas 4 for 10–12 minutes until lightly browned. Cool, then roughly chop 100 g of the nuts and set aside.

Put the remainder in a food processor or liquidizer and grind to a fine powder.

Mix the ground almonds in a mixing bowl with the flour, sugar and baking powder. Make a well in the centre. Beat the eggs with the yolk and the almond or vanilla essence and pour into the well. Gradually work the flour mixture into the eggs, then add the chopped almonds. Knead very well to bring the dough together – do not add any extra liquid.

Divide the dough in half and shape each piece into a flat log about 26 x 6 x 1.5 cm. Place the logs well apart on the baking sheet. Bake at 180°C (350°F) Gas 4 for about 25 minutes until golden and firm to the touch.

Remove from the oven and let cool for about 5 minutes. Reduce the oven temperature to 170°C (325°F) Gas 3. Transfer the logs to a cutting board then, using a serrated knife, gently and carefully cut them diagonally into slices about 1.5 cm thick. Arrange the slices, cut side up, on the baking sheet and bake for a further 10–12 minutes at 170°C (325°F) Gas 3 until golden and crisp.

Cool on a wire rack, then store in an airtight container and eat within 2 weeks.

*Traditional biscotti, flavoured with fennel seeds, are served as a digestif. This is a **modern** variation.*

cinnamon and raisin

biscotti

Put the almonds on a heatproof dish and toast in the oven for 10–12 minutes until lightly browned. Cool and leave whole. Whisk the egg, sugar and vanilla in a bowl, by hand or with an electric mixer, until very thick and pale (ribbons of mixture should trail from the whisk as you lift it out of the bowl). Sift the flour, baking powder, salt and cinnamon on to a piece of greaseproof paper, then sift again into the mixing bowl. Stir until thoroughly combined with the egg mixture, then stir in the raisins and almonds. Turn out on to the prepared sheet and shape it into a flat log about 26 x 6 x 1.5 cm. Bake the log in a preheated oven at 180°C (350°F) Gas 4 for 20–25 minutes or until golden brown. Let cool for about 5 minutes, or until firm, then transfer to a cutting board. With a serrated bread knife, cut the log on the diagonal into slices about 1 cm thick. Arrange on the sheet, and bake again for 10–15 minutes or until golden. Allow to rest for 5 minutes, then transfer to a wire rack to cool completely. Store in an airtight container and eat within 2 weeks.

Variation:

Chocolate Biscotti

Omit the raisins and cinnamon, add 50 g plain chocolate chunks with the almonds, and proceed as in the main recipe.

50 g whole blanched almonds

1 large egg

100 g golden caster sugar

1 teaspoon real vanilla essence

130 g plain flour

½ teaspoon baking powder

a pinch of salt

¾ teaspoon ground cinnamon

50 g raisins

a baking sheet, well greased

Makes about 20

*Tuiles are **perfect** with ice cream, creamy puddings or fruit salads.*
orange tuiles

Put the egg whites in a spotlessly clean, grease-free, non-plastic bowl. Using a hand or electric whisk, whisk slowly at first, then increase the speed until the egg whites form stiff peaks. Gradually whisk in the sugar, then the cooled melted butter and finally the sifted flour. If you use an electric mixer, keep it on low speed.

Gently stir in the grated orange rind and the liqueur, if using. Spoon 1 teaspoon of the mixture on to a prepared baking sheet and spread it into a thin disc about 10 cm across. Bake in a preheated oven at 180°C (350°F) Gas 4 for about 5 minutes or until it turns a very pale gold.

Remove from the oven and, using a palette knife, immediately loosen it from the sheet and drape over a rolling pin. It will harden very rapidly into a U-shape. Remove and set aside.

Once you have the knack, bake the tuiles 2 at a time. Store the tuiles in an airtight container, and eat within 2 days – humidity or damp makes them uncurl, so store with care. These biscuits are not suitable for freezing.

2 medium egg whites, at room temperature

120 g golden caster sugar

60 g unsalted butter, melted and cooled

60 g plain flour, sifted

the grated rind of

1 unwaxed orange

1 teaspoon orange liqueur (optional)

several baking sheets, greased

Makes about 18

A hint of cinnamon makes these delicate, lacy biscuits an excellent match for ice cream or creamy **summertime** *puddings.*

danish biscuits

150 g unsalted butter

150 g porridge oats

230 g golden caster sugar

2 medium eggs, beaten

1 tablespoon plain flour

2 teaspoons baking powder

1 teaspoon ground cinnamon

several baking sheets, well greased or lined with non-stick baking parchment

Makes about 24

Melt the butter gently in a medium saucepan. Remove from the heat and stir in the porridge oats. When thoroughly combined, add the remaining ingredients and mix well.

These biscuits are best baked in batches of three. (Cook the batches on one baking sheet while the other is cooling down). Space 3 mounds – each about 1 heaped teaspoonful of the mixture – well apart on a baking sheet.

Bake in a preheated oven at 180°C (350°F) Gas 4 for about 5–7 minutes or until golden brown.

Using a spatula, immediately lift the baked biscuits off the sheet and let cool upside down on a wire rack. Repeat the process until all the mixture is used.

These biscuits quickly lose their crispness in damp or humid conditions, so store carefully in an airtight container and eat within 4 days. They do not freeze well.

irish whiskey fingers

1 unwaxed lemon

100 g sultanas

80 ml whiskey

130 g unsalted butter,
at room temperature

130 g golden caster sugar

2 large eggs, separated

130 g self-raising flour

1–2 tablespoons demerara sugar

one 18 cm square cake tin,
greased and base-lined

Cuts into 10

Soak the fruit in whiskey the night before baking – Irish gives the best flavour, but Scotch is very good too.

Using a vegetable peeler, pare off the rind of the lemon and put in the bottom of a small bowl. Add the sultanas, then pour over the whiskey. Cover tightly and leave overnight.

With a wooden spoon or electric mixer, beat the butter until creamy. Beat in the sugar and continue beating until the mixture is very light and fluffy.

Beat in the egg yolks one at a time. Remove the lemon rind, then add the sultanas and whiskey to the cake mixture, carefully folding them in with a metal spoon.

In another bowl, whisk the egg whites until they form stiff peaks, then fold them into the mixture in 3 batches alternately with batches of the flour.

Spoon the mixture into the prepared tin and smooth the surface. Sprinkle with the demerara sugar, then bake in a preheated oven at 180°C (350°F) Gas 4 for about 25 minutes or until just firm to the touch.

Remove from the oven, let rest in the tin for about 5 minutes, then carefully unmould the cake on to a wire rack. Leave until completely cold, then cut into fingers.

Store in an airtight container and eat within 1 week, or freeze for up to 1 month.

For *authentic* taste, make these vanilla-scented French biscuits with unsalted best-quality butter.
sablés

Mix the flour, salt, icing sugar and diced butter in a food processor until the mixture resembles fine sand.
Add the egg yolks and vanilla and process again until the mixture comes together as a firm dough. Turn it out of the processor, wrap in clingfilm and chill for 15 minutes.
On a lightly floured work surface, roll out the chilled dough to about 5 mm thick, then cut out rounds with the fluted cutter.
Space them a little apart on the baking sheets.
Knead the trimmings together, roll again, cut more rounds and arrange them on the sheets. Brush the rounds very lightly with beaten egg, then chill for 15 minutes.
Brush again with the egg glaze, prick all over with a fork, then mark with the prongs to make a neat pattern.
Bake the biscuits in a preheated oven at 180°C (350°F) Gas 4 for 12–15 minutes or until golden brown.
Remove from the oven, leave on the baking sheets for a few seconds to firm up, then carefully transfer to a wire rack.
Let cool completely, then store in an airtight container and eat within 1 week, or freeze for up to 1 month.

200 g plain flour

a pinch of salt

80 g icing sugar

130 g unsalted butter, chilled and diced

3 egg yolks

½ teaspoon real vanilla essence

1 egg, beaten, to glaze

one 9 cm fluted biscuit cutter
several baking sheets, greased

Makes about 10

If using whole cardamom, crack the pods, remove the seeds and crush with a mortar and pestle.

sour cream
cardamom squares

250 g self-raising flour

½ teaspoon bicarbonate of soda

a pinch of salt

¼ teaspoon ground cardamom

170 g unsalted butter,
at room temperature

250 g golden caster sugar

3 large eggs

150 ml sour cream

icing sugar, for dusting

one 20 cm square cake tin,
greased and base-lined

Makes 9

Sieve the flour with the bicarbonate of soda, salt and ground cardamom, then set aside.

With a wooden spoon or electric mixer, cream the butter. Gradually beat in the sugar: continue beating until the mixture is very light and fluffy. Add the eggs one at a time, beating well after each addition. With a large metal spoon, fold in the flour mixture in 3 batches, alternating with the sour cream. Spoon the mixture into the prepared cake tin and smooth the surface. Bake in a preheated oven at 180°C (350°F) Gas 4 for about 45 minutes or until golden brown and firm to the touch. Loosen the edges with a round-bladed knife, then turn on to a wire rack. When completely cold, cut into 9 squares, and dust with icing sugar. Store in an airtight container and eat within 1 week, or freeze for up to 1 month.

mincemeat crumble

Sift the flour, salt and mixed spice into a mixing bowl. Rub in the diced butter with your fingertips until the mixture resembles fine crumbs. Stir in the sugar, diced apple, dried fruit and peel. Mix the egg and the milk, and stir them into the mixture to make a soft dough.

Spread the dough evenly in the prepared tin and sprinkle with the demerara sugar.

Bake in a preheated oven at 200°C (400°F) Gas 6 for about 20 minutes or until firm and golden. Remove from the oven, let cool for 1 minute, then cut into 9 squares. Let cool completely, then store in an airtight container, eat within 4 days, or freeze for up to 1 month.

Variation:

Dried Fruit, Pineapple and Apricot Crumble
Omit the apple and substitute 140 g of one of the luxury dried fruit mixtures, containing pineapple and apricot, that are often available around holiday time.

*Crisp, **tart**, eating apples are best for this quick and **easy** crumble.*

225 g self-raising flour

a pinch of salt

½ teaspoon ground mixed spice

85 g unsalted butter, chilled and diced

85 g unrefined demerara sugar

1 medium apple, peeled, cored and diced

100 g mixed dried fruit and peel

1 large egg

4 tablespoons milk

1–2 tablespoons demerara sugar

one 20 cm square cake tin, greased

Makes 9

57

pecan spice bars

90 g unsalted butter,
at room temperature

3 tablespoons golden syrup

1 large egg

180 g self-raising flour

a pinch of salt

¼ teaspoon grated nutmeg

½ teaspoon mixed ground spice

½ teaspoon ground cinnamon

¼ teaspoon ground ginger

90 g coarsely ground pecan nuts

1½ tablespoons milk

Spicy Pecan Topping:

2 tablespoons flour

2 tablespoons muscovado sugar

¼ teaspoon grated nutmeg

¼ teaspoon grated ginger

30 g unsalted butter, diced

30 g pecan halves

one 20 cm square cake tin,
greased and lined

Makes 15

Using a wooden spoon or electric mixer, cream the butter until light and fluffy. Beat in the golden syrup, then gradually beat in the egg.

Sift the flour with the salt and spices, then stir into the mixture together with the ground pecans and milk. When all the base ingredients are thoroughly combined, spoon the mixture into the prepared tin and smooth the surface.

To make the topping, first mix the flour with the sugar and spices. Work in the butter with your fingers to make small clumps of dough. Stir in the pecans.

Scatter the clumps over the base mixture in the tin, then bake in a preheated oven at 180°C (350°F) Gas 4 for about 25–30 minutes until firm to the touch.

Remove the cake in its paper lining from the tin. Let cool, then slice into 15 pieces. Store in an airtight container and eat within 1 week, or freeze up to 1 month.

An **excellent** combination of moist sponge base and *crunchy* topping of nuts and spices.

*Use only genuine maple syrup for a more **intense** flavour.*

maple syrup
pecan flapjacks

Heat the butter, sugar and syrup gently in a medium-sized saucepan, stirring occasionally, until dissolved. Remove from the heat, stir in the oats and nuts and mix well. Spread evenly in the prepared tin, pressing down lightly. Using a sharp knife, score the mixture into 10 rectangles. Bake in a preheated oven at 300°F (150°C) Gas 2 for about 25–30 minutes or until golden. Remove from the oven, and cut along the scored lines. Do not remove the flapjacks from the tin until they are completely cold. Store in an airtight container and eat within 1 week, or freeze for up to 1 month.

Variations:

Golden Syrup Flapjacks

Omit the pecan nuts and maple syrup, and use 1 tablespoon golden syrup instead. Instead of the nuts, add one of the following: 30 g raisins, 30 g chocolate pieces, 1 teaspoon ground ginger, 40 g each of chopped dates and walnut pieces, 40 g chopped almonds and a few drops almond essence, or 40 g chopped mixed nuts together with 40 g no-need-to-soak dried apricots.

150 g unsalted butter

120 g light brown muscovado sugar

1 tablespoon maple syrup

180 g porridge oats

70 g pecan nuts, roughly chopped

one 18 cm square cake tin, well-greased

Makes 10

tangy lemon bars

125 g plain flour

a pinch of salt

35 g icing sugar

100 g unsalted butter, chilled

3 drops real vanilla essence

Lemon Topping:

2 medium eggs

170 g golden caster sugar

the grated rind and juice
of 1 large unwaxed lemon

1 tablespoon plain flour

½ teaspoon bicarbonate of soda

icing sugar, for dusting

one 20 cm square cake tin,
well greased

Makes 12

Put the flour, salt and icing sugar into a food processor and combine well. Dice the butter and add to the processor with the vanilla. Process until the mixture comes together to make a firm dough.

Press the dough into the base of the prepared tin to make an even layer. Prick well with a fork and, if the weather is very warm, chill for 15 minutes.

Bake in a preheated oven at 180°C (350°F) Gas 4 for about 12–15 minutes until firm and slightly golden but not browned. Let cool in the tin while making the topping.

Using an electric mixer or whisk, whisk the eggs in a bowl until frothy. Gradually whisk in the sugar and continue until the mixture is thick and foamy. Whisk in the lemon rind and juice, then the flour and bicarbonate of soda. Pour the mixture over the base and bake for 20–25 minutes until it turns golden brown.

Let cool in the tin, then divide into 12 rectangles.

Store in an airtight container and eat within 4 days. This recipe does not freeze well.

A crisp, buttery base with a sticky topping and a sharp citrus tang.

a
almond:
    biscotti 44
    crescents 30

b
baking sheets 8
biscotti:
    almond 44
    chocolate 45
    cinnamon and raisin 45
butter, unsalted 7

c
cardamom, sour cream, squares 56
chocolate 8
    bitter chocolate butter biscuits 28
    shortbread 25
    mocha macaroons 35
    white chocolate and macadamia
      nut crumbles 38
cinnamon and raisin biscotti 45
coffee:
    espresso walnut squares 32
    mocha macaroons 35
Cornish fairings 16
cranberries, dried 13
crumbles:
    mincemeat, 57
    dried fruit 57
    white chocolate and macadamia
      nut 38

d
Danish biscuits 48
dried fruit crumble 57

e
eggs 7
electric food mixers 6

f
flapjacks, maple syrup pecan 61
flours 7

g
ginger shortbread 22
gingernuts, old-fashioned 14

i
Irish whiskey fingers 50

l
lace biscuits 29
lemon:
    lemon bars, tangy 62
    lemon poppy seed biscuits 18
    lemon zest 8

m
maple syrup pecan flapjacks 61
mocha macaroons 35

n
nuts 7
    almond crescents 30
    espresso walnut squares 32
    lace biscuits 29
    maple syrup pecan flapjacks 61
    mocha macaroons 35
    peanut butter and jelly sandwich
      biscuits 36
    pecan spice bars 58
    walnut biscuits 40
    white chocolate macadamia nut
      crumbles 38

o
oat and raisin biscuits 13
old-fashioned gingernuts 14
orange tuiles 47

orange zest 8
ovens 9

p
peanut butter and jelly sandwich
    biscuits 36
pecan spice bars 58
poppy seed, lemon, biscuits 18

r
raisin, cinnamon and, biscotti 45

s
sablés 53
scales 8
shelf positions 9
shortbreads:
    chocolate 25
    demerara 23
    Grasmere ginger 22
    pistachio 23
sour cream cardamom squares 56
spoons, measuring 8
sugar 7

t
tangy lemon bars 62
thermometer, oven 9
tuiles, orange 47

v
vanilla 8

w
walnut biscuits 40
wheaten biscuits 12
whiskey, Irish 50
whisky, Scotch 50
white chocolate and macadamia
    nut crumbles 38